The Bible fo

GW00854834

11 Easy **Steps** to Understanding the Bible & Becoming Closer to Christ in the Process...

Julia Bristol

Copyright

Table of Contents

INTRODUCTION

This book contains proven steps and strategies on how to understand the most important book ever written in man's history – the Bible.

I have written this special book with you in mind. Dedicating a daily time with God and cultivating an intimate relationship with Him is made possible by taking the time to read His Word. Not many people find the Bible easy to read and understand. Some are caught up with their busy schedules, while there are those who just skim through the pages without really contemplating on His Word. If you are one of those who are trap in this Bible reading dilemma, now is the best time to rethink and start a daily commitment to read the Word of God.

This may not come easy as hesitations like "How do I get started", "I find it hard to understand the Bible", or "I don't have time" will naturally come into mind. If you feel as though you are lost or you have been reading for quite some time now but nothing seems to be happening, I want to assure you that God can help you shift to the right direction. He will give you wisdom and understanding if you seek Him with all your heart.

In this book, you will learn step by step process to aid you in your reading and get to know the Lord Jesus Christ more.

Thanks again for downloading this book, I hope you enjoy it!

Julia

Chapter 1 – Step 1 – Introduction to the Holy Bible

The Bible is considered as the most popular book ever written and remains at the top spot of the bestselling books. But what really is the Bible? How did people come to have their Bibles? And how can we understand this book that claims to be the Word of God?

What is the Bible?

The word Bible comes from the Greek word "biblos or biblion meaning book. Its plural form of biblos is biblia (books). This is but an apt meaning since the Bible is deemed as a library on its own, with two main sections (The Old Testament and the New Testament). But more notable than the origin of its name is the divine source.

What Does the Bible Mean to Humans and What Does God Want from His People?

The Bible was written as a constant reminder that God desires to establish a relationship with us. He longs a relationship so close that He created us in His own image and likeness. He first demonstrated His love for His creations when even if Adam and Eve disobeyed Him, He still pursued them. This alone demonstrates what is central in God's heart – us. Believe it or not, He thinks of your welfare and guides you every step of the way. Although it may be hard to believe knowing that a Great and Almighty God chose to humble himself through Jesus Christ considering how little and sinful we are, but He still did. What's amazing? Despite people's imperfections and shortcomings, God chose to reveal Himself through the Bible.

God Wanted to Make Himself Known

The humility of the Lord is so overwhelming that He was the one who initiated a relationship with His people. The Bible testifies to the many events and ways He has done this. He revealed himself to Abraham, Moses, the prophets, and many others. His miraculous acts were evident in the history of Israel and even made a covenant with the Israelites. How can you forget the parting of the Red Sea and the plagues? Above all, He sent Jesus Christ, His only begotten son, who died on the cross so that many people will live and will experience eternity with God. Jesus is the ultimate revelation of the Almighty in Heaven.

The Accounts of God and His People

All the accounts of God's miraculous works, His people and their inspiring stories are all recorded and compiled in what people now know and read as the Bible. Through the guidance and inspiration of the Holy Spirit, authors of the books of the Bible, although came from human words, also became the very words of God. Thus, one can fairly say that in this book, God has made Himself known, revealed His intentions, will, and love for mankind. This makes the Bible the very foundation of a Christian's life. Your life should be anchored to the Word of God. That is why it is important that you understand the context of the Bible.

How Can We Understand What the Bible Says?

God, being the best communicator, knows that in order for Him to speak to His people, He has to enter into their language and culture. The Bible goes beyond time and space and was able to speak to people of different race, generations, periods and culture. The Bible was handed down from generation to generation – first to the Israelites then to the early church. In order to understand the Bible, you would need to have a knowledge about the following:

The Different Languages Used in the Bible

The Process of Translation

The Genres in the Bible

The Context of the Reader

The Different Languages of the Bible

The Old Testament was written in Hebrew and was later on translated to Greek. On the other hand, the New Testament, from its beginning, was written in Greek as well. Among the many translations of the Bible, the Latin and Syriac versions were the most significant of all. This is because these two have become the bases for the many translations that came later on. For thousands of years, the Bible was read in Latin until one brave man by the name of William Tyndale translated the Bible into

English that resulted to his execution (he was hanged and burned to death).

What is the significance of knowing all these? Because there are times when people take the Bible for granted not knowing that it has gone through many translations and the people behind it had taken much sacrifice before the Bible came to us. It is important to understand the process of translation so that you are better trained in reading the Bible.

So how was the Bible translated into the English language?

The Process of Translation

Translation is comprise of two variables: the origin or the source language and the receptor language. In this case, it originated from the Hebrew language and translated into English. Translation can be done in two ways. First is through Formal equivalence or one that aims for word for word correspondence wherein the original context is preserved as much as possible in the translation. And the other one is Dynamic equivalence wherein it attempts to communicate the original context into how the receptor language would render it.

The Genres in the Bible

Why is there a need to understand this? Knowledge of the different types of genres in the Bible will give readers tips on what the authors want to communicate. The following are some of the genres you will get to read in the Bible: narrative, history, prophecy, gospels, poetry, letters, laws and apocalyptic writings.

The Context of the Reader

To fully understand the Bible, a Christian wanting to know the Word of God must need to be aware of their preconceived ideas. People approach their Bibles with their own set of beliefs and experiences. Although there is nothing wrong with this, the important thing is that you know where you are coming from. Fully understanding the context of the Bible requires an open mind and heart. A person must be humble enough to take the path where the truth is leading him.

The Ultimate Goal of Reading the Bible

That is to encounter the main author of the Bible – God.

Remember that you approach this book not to be informed, but to be changed as you encounter God through His Word. As you go through your everyday journey of reading His Word, may you be reminded that more than anything else, God wants a relationship with you. He aspires for you to know His Word and reveal His plans for your life. More importantly, He is just a prayer away. In order to experience all these, God has one wish: that you must be willing to listen to His voice and obey His call. No matter how difficult the challenge may seem or how dark your sin appears, remember that God loves you and only wants what is best for you.

Chapter 2 – Step 2 - Get to Know Your Bible More

In order to fully understand the Bible and increase your reading time, it is important to learn more about its parts, individual books, and genres.

The Bible encompasses 66 individual books in different eras of history, by different authors and writing styles, all for the purpose of reaching out to Christians walking in Christian faith and would like to follow Jesus and know Him more.

What made the Bible distinct from other anthologies is that it was meticulously written by a team of scholars and translators in their commitment to the Bible as God's divine Word in written form. As you read God's Word, may you be reminded that it sheds light to the darkest of paths, answers your deepest longings and questions, and most importantly, paves the way to the good's final destination – eternity.

Books of the Law

These are from Genesis through Deuteronomy. These first five books of the Bible is where God reveals himself as compassionate, merciful, holy, and just. God's interaction with his creations has been the highlight of these books. He dealt with the Israelites, His chosen people, and made himself known to other different people in the Bible. Written in these books is how God wants His people to live and expects to rule their lives. He rewards obedience and punishes the wicked.

Books of History

These are from Joshua through Esther. The books highlight the history of the Israelites and some notable women at that time. These are an account of the Israelites' relationship with the Lord. A familiar pattern experienced up to this day - God expects obedience from his people; people would reject His discipline and turn to their evil ways; soon these evil deeds will be recognized and they would ask forgiveness from the Lord; God accepts and forgives, and restore His fellowship with His people. The pattern rejection-reprimand-repentance-restoration is evident up until now.

Books of Poetry

These are from Job through Song of Songs. These books tackle about people's hardship and struggles as manifested in Job's life. These books likewise touched on the unending subject about suffering and misery. However, you will also read about God's wisdom and how one can never fathom the ways and thinking of the infinite God. These books also taught the kind of worship considered pleasing to the Lord.

Books of the Prophets

These are from Isaiah through Malachi. God has shown so much compassion to His people that he uses prophets to give directives and make His plans and intentions known to all. These books also aimed to the most awaited Messiah, Jesus Christ. The One who died and restored humans' relationship with God.

Books of History

These are from Matthew through Acts. These account the life of Jesus Christ and how He proclaimed the Good News together with His disciples and followers. It is through these books where you will see the establishment of the church, Jesus' bride and body on Earth.

Letters

These are from Romans through Revelations. You will read about letters addressed to church leaders and believers. The doctrine of faith and the responsibilities of being a believer are all highlighted in these books.

Chapter 3 – Step 3 - Familiarize Yourself with Some of the Most Important Books in the Bible

The Old Testament

Genesis

Genesis serves as the foundation for the entire Bible. The word Genesis comes from the Greek word meaning "beginning". This book is about beginnings – the beginning of the world and the beginning of human race. It is likewise known to be the book of faith as it is mainly concerned of who God is, His power, and how He has been involved in the lives of His creations. The creation narratives state the existence of God and how all life here on earth originated from Him.

The following are stories you can expect to read from the book of Genesis:

The story of Adam and Eve where the consequences of sin are clearly seen.

The story of Cain and Abel that teaches what greediness and hatred could bring.

The destruction of Sodom and Gomorrah, and the story of Noah.

The salvation of Noah and his family, Lot, and Jacob.

The story of Joseph from the pastureland of Canaan to the palace of Egypt.

The story of Abraham whom God promised descendants as numerous as the stars in heaven.

A faithful reading of the book of Genesis will show you the wonders of God, His power, His ever loving nature. It will take you on a journey of close encounter with the owner of the sky, the creator of the universe, and the God of history.

Exodus

Exodus comes from the Greek word meaning exit. This recounts the story of Moses and his involvement in the two of the most important events in the history of the Bible and the people of Israel. The two key events – the exodus from Egypt and the giving of the Ten Commandments at Mount Sinai – are proof that God is faithful in keeping His promises of protecting those who believe in Him. And although the plagues that came to the Egyptians were sent by God, the laws He gave the Israelites were meant for them to maintain harmonious relationship with the Lord after they had been delivered from slavery and carried on to the promise land.

Job

The book of Job deals with troubles and human suffering. It tells the story of a man who was faithful to God and refuses to do evil. He was blessed with many children, good health and much wealth. But when Job loses everything, the book then focused as to why such a faithful servant of the Lord, someone who is righteous in every way like Job has to suffer. Job's friends tried to answer questions like: Does God cause people to suffer? Does He really care? Is suffering caused by human sin?

The book of Job challenges its readers to discover that the mysterious power and ways of the Lord are beyond understanding. Reading this book will dare you to bare your heart before God. Notice how easy it is to offer your thanks and praise to the Lord, but find it hard to offer the many confusing questions and emotions in your hearts. But despite all these, it is only God whom can satisfy your cries and provide comfort.

These were only three of the most remarkable books you can read from the Old Testament. Some of the other books include Leviticus, Numbers, Deuteronomy, Joshua, Judges, Ruth, Samuel, Kings, Chronicles, Ezra, Nehemiah, Tobit, Judith, Esther, Maccabees, Job, Psalms, Proverbs, Ecclesiastes, Song of Songs, wisdom of Solomon, Sirach, Isaiah, Jeremiah, Lamentations, Baruch, Ezekiel, Daniel, Josea, Joel, Amos, Jonah and many more.

The New Testament

The books from the New Testament talks about Jesus' teachings. The books stress that Jesus is the fulfillment of the Old Testament prophecy. Some of the remarkable books include:

Matthew

This is intended to teach Christians what is expected of them as a follower of Jesus Christ. The gospel of Matthew was written to strengthen the faith of those experiencing persecution. It teaches Christians not to give up on their faith, but instead see persecution as an opportunity to spread the Good News to all nations. Matthew also presents teachings from Jesus Christ with emphasis on discipleship. The Gospel is intended to teach Christians what is expected of them when they decide to carry the cross, follow Jesus, and lead a new way of life with God.

Mark

This may be the shortest among the gospels, but is considered the most powerful. Mark represents the Good News about Jesus Christ. First, his miracle-working powers demonstrated that He really is the Son of God. Second, the people who chose to follow Jesus must be willing to walk the same road as His. As Mark 8:34 said, "If any of you want to be my followers, you must forget about yourself. You must take up your cross and follow me."

John

Of all the Gospels in the New Testament, John was considered one of the most focused on demonstrating that Jesus Christ is God. It is so special that throughout the Gospel, Jesus is called the "Word", Jesus repeatedly use the words "I am" in describing Himself, and John narrates the many miracles Jesus has done. Why was the Gospel of John written? The answer is simple – "But these are written so that you will put your faith in Jesus and the Messiah and the Son of God. If you have faith in Him, you will have true life."

These were only 3 of the many gospels and books of the New Testament. Some of the other gospels include Acts, Romans, Corinthians, Galatians, Ephesians, Philippians, Colossians, Thessalonians, and Timothy among others.

Chapter 4 – Step 4 - Overview of the Scriptures

Dedicating your time and effort to really understand the Bible can be very hard especially for those who just started on their journey towards reading the Good News. The 4th step is to familiarize yourself with the scriptures. Know what to look through given your present situation or circumstances in life. Feed your faith and begin acquainting yourself with some of the Bible verses you can run to (and even memorize) whether in good times or in bad.

When in sorrow, John 14 has the most comforting of verses that would surely make you want to cry. God's Word offers a deep sense of comfort, something that you will not easily find elsewhere.

"Do not let your hearts be troubled, Trust in God; trust in Me. In my Father's house are many rooms; if it were so, I would have told you."

When you worry, Matthew 6:25 will remind you to think of your worries less. The Lord has promised that He will take care of you and your every need if you just put your trust in Him.

"Therefore, I tell you, do not worry about your life, what you will eat or drink; or about your boy, what you will wear. Is not life more important than food, and the body more important than clothes?"

When you are in danger, Psalm 91 offers an assurance that God is with you every step of the way so that no harm will ever befall on you and your whole household.

"He who dwells in the shelter of the Most High will rest in the shadow of the Almighty. I will say of the Lord, "He is my refuge and my fortress, my God, in whom I trust."

When God seems so distant, Psalm 139 offers a sigh of relief knowing that He is there and He knows your heart. You may never know the reason why He seems so far away, and yet you can take comfort from this verse.

"O Lord, you have searched me and you know me. You know when I sit and when I rise; you perceive my thoughts from afar. You discern my going out and my lying down; you are familiar with all my ways."

When your faith needs steering, Hebrews 11 offers a refresher. There will be times when your faith will eventually bend. Times when you wanted to do things your way. And times when your ways are not aligned in His will. When faced with this kind of predicament, know that this verse provides clarity.

"Now faith is being sure of what we hope for and certain of what we do not see. This is what the ancients were commanded for. By faith we understand that the universe was formed at God's command, so that what is seen is not what made of what was visible."

When bitterness get the better of you, it would do you good to read through 1 Corinthians 13: 4-7 and be made whole again. And know that love is all that matters in the end. Afterall, isn't God love?

"Love is patient, love is kind. It does not envy, it does not boast, it is not proud. It is not rude, it is not self-seeking, it is not easily angered, it keeps no record of wrongs. Love does not delight in evil but rejoices with the truth. It always protects, always trusts, always hopes always perseveres."

When you feel down and out, this Bible verse from Romans 8:28 will definitely help in picking the shattered pieces of your heart. It would make you realize that God has good plans for you.

"And we know that in all things God works for the good of those who love him, who have been called according to His purpose."

When you feel lonely and fearful, what better way to wipe those tears away by feeding your soul from verses of Psalm 23. Keeping the verse by heart will surely make you want to just rest in the Lord. For truly, He is your peace in this chaotic world.

"The Lord is my shepherd, I shall not be in want. He makes me lie down in green pastures, He leads me

beside quiet waters, He restores my soul. He guides me in paths pf righteousness, for His name's sake. Even though I walk through the valley of the shadow of death, I will fear no evil for You are with me; Your rod and Your staff, they comfort me."

When you are bothered and do not know what to do, the Lord has Exodus 4:11 prepared for you. He created you and therefore worthy of your praise. He is all powerful, and there is nothing He cannot do for you.

"The Lord said to him, "Who gave man his mouth? Who makes him deaf or mute? Who gives him sight or make him blind? Is it not I, the Lord?"

When you feel you are lacking in things, remember that God is generous. He hears your cry and is sensitive to your needs. He cares for you, especially those who are in need of His mercy. And, it is displayed in Deuteronomy 24:19.

"When you are harvesting in your field and you overlook a sheaf, do not go back to get it. Leave it to the alien, the fatherless, and the widow."

When you feel unloved and uncared for, always remember that He is a compassionate God. He loves and cares for you. He is ever present in all the happenings in your life. 2 Chronicles 30:9 is a beautiful verse to live by.

"If you return to the Lord, then your brothers and your children will be shown compassion by their captors and will come back to this land, for the Lord your God is gracious and compassionate."

When you feel hopeless and could no longer hold on to your present situation, know that you have a God who gives hope. As Isaiah 9:6 best describes Jesus –

"for to us a child is born, to us a son is given, and the government will be on his shoulders. And he will be called Wonderful Counselor, Mghty God, Everlasting Father, Prince of Peace."

When you wanted to have the greatest gift of all, know that accepting Jesus Christ in your life as your Lord and Savior is the most precious of all gifts that no material possession could ever replace. And this is made evident when God the Father has sent forth Jesus Christ to save mankind. John 3:16-17 beautifully narrates:

"For God so loved the world, that He gave His only begotten Son, that whoever believes in Him shall not perish, but have eternal life. 17"For God did not send the Son into the world to judge the world, but that the world might be saved through Him...."

Chapter 5 – Step 5 - Set a Private Time Each Day to Spend with God

The church is Jesus' bride. Marriage's symbolism is applied to Jesus and the body of believers. In the New Testament, Jesus, the Bridegroom, has chosen the church to become His bride. Similar today, the betrothal period during the biblical times was that the bride and groom were separated from each other until they walk down the aisle and wed, so is the bride of Christ, separated from His bridegroom. Now, the Church, as the bride, has the responsibility to be faithful to Him. When is the wedding? It will take place in the Second Coming of the Lord Jesus Christ. Such beautiful union of finally being one – Christ and His bride, the Church, an Eternal Union in Heaven.

All these, you will eventually know and understand if you read the Bible. And, what better way to fully understand the Word of God but to belong in a Church and be with other believers. The significance? You will get to have an in-depth understanding of the Scriptures you find confusing and be able to get the opinion of other believers and even the elders to shed light on some grey areas.

The following are some of the benefits of being a Church member as you continue to walk faithfully with Jesus and know His word:

1. Personal and spiritual development – Becoming a member of a church helps in your development as an individual. The church offers discipleship and spiritual development. You no longer be reading and reflecting on the Bible alone, you have the Church to guide you through every step of the way.

2. You get to join a small group – this is similar to having not just Bible buddies but also a spiritual family where you expect to grow more in the likeness of Jesus. The good thing about focused groups is that it is way easier to reach your goals of fully understanding the Bible and get to know God more because you are surrounded by people who have the same goals as yours.

3. A deep sense of belongingness – the church identifies you as a believer in Jesus Christ. As the Apostle Paul has written in his letter to the Ephesians, ""You are no longer strangers

and foreigners. You are citizens along with all of God's holy people. You are members of God's family." – Ephesians 2:19. With a deep sense of belongingness comes distinction. As a believer in Jesus Christ, you are different in the sense that you are committed to Christ's bride as evident to your being a member of the church. Along with becoming a member of the church is to personally confess your faith in the Lord Jesus, to be baptized in water and openly identify yourself as one with Christ. A church's membership is like saying, "I'm serious with my walk with the Lord and I'm not ashamed of claiming the one and only begotten son, Jesus Christ as my Lord and Savior."

4. You get to have encouragement like no other – Your walk with the Lord is not always a bed of roses, there will be times when you will falter. Even godly Christians and those who have been walking with the Lord for many years still experience spiritual dryness. It is but

normal, as we are only humans. But know that when you are a member of a church, its main role is to provide continuous encouragement to believers in living life on a daily basis. It is not just about getting by each day, but getting as much as you can out of the situation given you. If you have a spiritual family, you are assured that you will have a hand to pull you up when spiritual drought comes and arms to help keep you going. When you get tired pf reading the Bible, you have a church to provide encouragement and light to just keep reading and moving forward. As I Corinthians 12:4-7 would put it "A spiritual gift is given to each of us as a means of helping the entire church."

5. You are offered spiritual protection – Admit it, the world you live in is filled with evil ways. People now shifted their priorities to worldly matters and guarding their souls has not become a top priority. When you belong to a church and the Bible has become your basis to living, you are assured that there will be people who will watch over your soul and will keep you on the right track. One of the church's goals is to keep a close watch at your

soul. As the Apostle Paul said, "As each part does its own special work, it helps the other parts grow...."

6. A church helps you develop a Christ-like attitude – with the Bible as your guide and your Church as your spiritual support, developing a Christ-like attitude is achievable. A true follower of Jesus no longer lives for himself, but for the good of others. You become selfless and no longer concern yourself with personal issues. Instead, you become more aware of other's needs and welfare.

As true believers and followers of Jesus, it is not enough that we read the Bible, but it is also of prime importance that you read and understand His word together with your fellow believers.

As believers in Christ, we, the church, considered as the bride of Jesus, wait on great anticipation that soon we will be reunited with our Bridegroom, just as He promised. Until then, we remain faithful to Him, fulfill His purpose in our lives, and become like Him 'till we become one with the Lord for all eternity.

Chapter 6 – Step 6 - Pray

One can never underestimate the power of prayer. It is so powerful that it can move mountains. As Isaiah 64:1 put it, "Oh, that you would rend the heavens and come down, that the mountains would tremble before you."

Prayer links us to God who is all-powerful. When you put your hands together in prayer, you open your communication line with the Creator of Heaven and Earth, your Almighty Father.

If you wanted to build a stronger and more intimate relationship with Jesus, you should make praying a lifestyle. And so the care you give in your daily routine begs this question. How much time do you devote each day to get ready spiritually and nourish your soul each morning? Do you read the scriptures, and meditate what you have read day and night? Or, do you worry more about getting out the door and start your day right away than the condition of your hearts?

If you really wanted to understand the Bible and develop a nurturing relationship with God, prayer must be in the top list of your priority in life. Pray before you begin reading the Word of God. Pray about the verses you do not quite understand, and ask Him to give you wisdom and guidance through the help of the Holy Spirit.

When you pray before reading the Bible, remember that God is worthy of your praise – Praise God for who He is, for what He has done for you, and is doing in your life.

The question now is, when is the best time to pray? As Thessalonians 5:16-18 said, "Be joyful always; pray continually; give thanks in all circumstances, for this is God's will for you in Christ Jesus. In other words, pray without ceasing. This does not mean nonstop talking. It must be a recurring prayer, and so one must always be in an attitude of prayer.

While the best time to come to God in prayer greatly depends upon the person, it will still be helpful to know recommended times to pray:

- *In the morning* – Give thanks to the Lord for He has given you another day to live. Starting your day with a prayer is fuel to your soul. An early morning prayer is recommended because it hints the conscience that it is the first order of the day. A morning meeting with God is your first blow as you battle through the day. Do not wait until you are all consumed. Remember that Satan will do everything, even good things, just to shut out prayer in your mornings. Besides, a prayer that is put off during the latter part of the day never happens.

- *When you are down and do not know what to do* – Problems are normal occurrences. Oftentimes, it brings you to the edge without a clue of what to do next. Whenever faced with this kind of situation, prayer is a good resolve. You might not get the answers right away, and oftentimes do not, but the assurance that God listens is more than enough to make you feel better and move forward.

- *When about to read the Word of God* – Pray before you open the Bible and read the Scriptures. Ask God to help you understand every word and receive it in your life. Remember that as you open the Bible, you are entering into His presence. So make every effort to approach Him in a bold yet humble manner.

- *Evening Prayer* – Just as you would begin the day well, it is of equal importance to end it just right. The graces bestowed upon you in the course of the day, and the protection you need as you sleep through the night are just enough reasons to submit yourself to God and give thanks to Him.

After you pray, take a moment to reflect, wait in openness, and get yourself ready to receive God. While you contemplate on what you have prayed to God, ask yourself the following questions:

- What does God want to tell me?

- What does God the Father, Son and the Holy Spirit wanted to reveal of himself?

- What insight does God want to tell me? Is there a warning to heed? What does He require of me at the moment?

Those questions will serve as your guide as you reflect and uncover God's message for you through prayer and meditation.

Just as praying before reading the Word of God is important, it must also be your way of life. A person who sincerely comes to God in prayer is never turned away.

He even hears those who bargain with Him. You may find yourself in a situation like this, "Lord if you will just deliver me from this trouble, I promise to fully surrender to your will." But of course, all those are mere promises and humans tend to go back to their old ways once they get what they've asked for.

When you find yourself unwilling to submit to God, pray. When you find it hard to obey His commands, pray. And when you think you can no longer hold on and felt guilty of all your shortcomings, pray.

The following are reasons why prayer should be a way of life:

1. Prayer keeps your mind and thoughts set on Christ – God could have programmed you for failure and defeat if He wanted to, but He didn't. You may not feel worthy, but God views you as one. He created you to be a person of extreme worth not because of what you have done, but because of what Christ has done for you. When you keep this in mind as you pray, you will feel that your life is hidden in Christ – a place of security and highest value.

2. Prayer teaches us to trust in the Lord's will and plan for our lives – Through prayer, you come to accept God's purpose for your life. You come to the realization that if your goals and purpose are not aligned in God's will, you will always have a sense of longing for something you don't even know about. Prayer will make you realize that you no longer have to strive for significance for you already received the most important gift of all – Jesus Christ and His unconditional love.

3. Prayer gives you a deep and abiding love for His Word – It is much easier to study the Bible if you come to God and ask for His guidance. When you empty yourself for the Lord, it is when He fills you with knowledge and wisdom of His Word.

4. Prayer increases your faith – It is easy to become discouraged or overwhelmed by circumstances in life. There are times when you feel you are stuck in life making it hard for you to deal with everyday challenges. In

the Bible, the apostles' faith were shattered after the crucifixion of Jesus Christ. But God did not leave them in a hopeless situation. Instead, He motivates them to move forward and continue to spread the Good News. When you apply this in your life, you will notice that you are gradually transformed into a man of faith. Although this may not happen overnight, the journey towards this realization is definitely worth taking.

5. Prayer brings you home in God's embrace.

Isn't it overwhelming to just be with God in silence and feel the warmth of his embrace? Praying is not just about you doing the talking. It should also be listening to what God has to say to you. As you listen to His voice, feel the overwhelming peace of just being with His presence as you pray. Now, that is really refreshing and something to look forward to everyday!

Chapter 7 – Step 7 - Keep Your Relationship with God Intact while Studying His Word

Many people miss out on God's ocean of blessings because they thought they can do it all. They rely on their strength and hard work. Lack of peace usually indicates that there is a problem. It is either you are unwilling to submit yourself wholly to God or the enemy is distracting and seeking to reroute you away from God's best. Just as Peter reminded us that the devil "prowls around like a roaring lion, seeking to devour." (1 Peter 5:8.

So what can you do to keep your relationship intact with the Lord?

Check your heart and make sure your first desire is to really follow God and not your own worldly desires. The Bible is clear when it said in Matthew 6:33, "But seek first the kingdom of God and his righteousness, and all these things will be added to you." Far too many people probably fail on this. In your effort to seek financial freedom and a good life for your family, your focus tends to be on how you will keep your life convenient. Many people fail to seek God because they are too busy seeking other things. They assume that either He will approve of all they are doing or He will exempt them of His rules.

What you should do:

In everything you do, put God first. This may be easier said than done, but if you just try to keep your focus on Jesus and eternity, earthly things will surely come least to your priorities.

*Trust the Lord even if it means giving up things, opportunities, or even people in your life.

At times, the Lord allows your faith to be tested not to make you suffer from sins you have committed as many people thought of, but to strengthen and prepare you for the next step in life. As you read the Bible, you will encounter people whom God have tested.

- Job was severely tested when God took away his family and wealth.

- Joseph was sent in prison for a crime he did not commit.

- David was resigned on running away from a man bent on killing him.

But what do they have in common? They've remained faithful. When difficulty comes, you have a choice to look at it in two ways – either as a road towards a more intact relationship with the Lord or a road that is set for destruction.

Never be afraid to ask God to show you the way

There will be inescapable situations in life. Along the way, you will experience, defeat, rejection, sorrow, and a loss of a loved one among others. But this shouldn't stop you from seeking God. Untoward situations happening in your life should not be points of failure. Instead, they should be avenues for hope and blessings. As you read the Bible, turn it to Isaiah 40:29, *"God gives strength to the weary, and to him who lacks might, He increases power."*

Ask God to help you make wise decisions

Be humble enough to admit that you cannot do all things without God's help – even by making your own decisions in life. Living an abundant life is only attainable in knowing God. Everything is encompassed in this. You can find Solomon's inspiring choice when God asked him for his wish.

"In Gibeon, the Lord appeared to Solomon in a dream; and God said: "Ask what you wish Me to give you." Then Solomon said, "You have shown great loving kindness to your servant David my father, according as he walked before You in truth and in righteousness and uprightness of heart... so give your servant an understand heart to judge your people to discern between good and evil." 1 Kings 3:5-6, 9

What you should do:
Stop thinking about what you could have acquired or how much you could have saved and invested in the bank. In God's economy, riches are found in knowing

God and having intimate relationship with Him. When you dedicate your life to Him, He will give you all the things you need, even the wisdom to discern what is right from wrong. Afterall, the loving God's very character is wisdom.

Allow God to have His way in you

Remember that making decisions based solely on the opinion of others or the facts laid before you could spell disaster in the long run. Of course, you will receive godly advices from family and friends, but sometimes, God wants you to seek Him first and know His say in the situation you are in before seeking other's opinion.

What you should do:

Read the Bible and ask God to speak through His Word. Ask God to direct you to the way He wanted you to take. If you seek God with all your heart, you will never feel restless in your decisions, and you will instantly feel that God is taking the wheel.

Chapter 8 – Step 8 - Attend Bible Studies

A Christian with a desire to know the Truth must be avid. Knowing God's Word, understanding what is written, and applying the teachings in the Bible must be in his topmost priority in life.

What is the importance of attending Bible studies in your desire to understand the Bible and get to know Jesus more? Read on and be encouraged to finally say "yes" to study the Word of God with your brothers and sisters in Christ.

1. The Bible is your source of knowledge – The only way you will get to know the living God is by reading and studying the Bible. When talks about spiritual things, remember that there is no such thing as love at first sight. It does not work that way. A believer of Christ must work hard each day to get to know Jesus and make every effort to build an intimate relationship with Him. Understanding the context of the Bible requires a daily dose of God's Word. As 1 Cor. 2:16 put it,

   "For who has known the mind of the Lord that he

may instruct him? But we have the mind of Christ."

2. Bible studies create an uplifting environment –

    The reason why many Christians find it helpful to study the Word of God with their peers is because the feeling is overwhelming. When you see people who are earnestly seeking for God just as you do, you feel all the more inspired and motivated. You get excited knowing that you can draw inspiration and encouragement from these people. You are assured that as you study the Bible, you will continuously reap insights from different people's testimonies.

3. You take one step in building truth into your life - When you spend time studying His Word, you will learn more about Jesus through the help of the Holy Spirit and studying together lets you share stories about how Jesus redeemed you and how He is working in your life and using you to touch other's lives and ultimately become a blessing to others.

4. A renewed fellowship with the Lord – The psalmist writes, *"Your Word I have treasured in my heart,*

*that I may not sin against You. "*God's spirit will teach you more about Him. Sin will become less of a temptation because you will finally realize that Sin only leads to disappointment, sadness and brokenness. Notice the time when you were not as conscious with the effects of sin? You were made to believe that you will not suffer for your disobedience, but you surely will. Remember the after-effects of sin is a broken fellowship with the Lord. But now that you are studying the Bible, you will be more cautious of your actions and decisions.

5. Bible studies create fellowship among believers –

   According to Matthew 18:20, *'For where two or three have gathered together in My name, I am there in their midst. "* Studying the Bible together makes for a stronger faith and prayer. Christ promises to be present in the midst of His people gathering together in His name. It implies, Jesus' omniscience and omnipresence. This is considered a blessing on united prayer.

Chapter 9 – Step 9 - Understand Bible Stories and Relate Them to Your Life Experiences

Imagine this typical scenario: As you go through your everyday duties and responsibilities, how many times have you barely given God a second thought? You were so focused on achieving things you believe will give you a sense of importance and recognition. You feel as if you are moving forward when in reality, you're not. Now, you're on the state of asking yourself, "Why did God allow this to happen?", "What went wrong?"

You may be going through tough roads, but one thing is for sure, no matter the circumstances that you are going through right now, God is aware of your greatest need. He knows every disappointment and frustration, and He knows that weariness could be headed your way if you fail to set the focus on Him. As the prophet Isaiah wrote, *"The Lord will continually Guide you , and satisfy your desire in scorched places, and give strength to your bones; and you will be like a watered garden, and like a spring of water whose waters do not fail."(58:11).*

The Bible is filled with stories that you can relate to. Start reading today and get to know the stories of the greatest people in the Bible and how you can learn from them as you go through your everyday life and walk with the Lord.

The Book of Ruth

This book is considered as one of the beautiful stories you will read in the Bible. It teaches us that God's purpose in your life is sometimes revealed in unexpected ways. Believe that God works in the lives of those who are faithful to Him. God's goodness is for everyone and He is at work in their everyday lives.

There are only two books in the Old Testament written after a woman's name. One is Ruth and the other is Esther. This is an inspiring story of a woman, a Moabitess, who left her country just to be with her husband and his family. Naomi was Ruth's mother in law. After her husband and sons had died, Naomi decided to go back to her homeland and Ruth decided to go with her. The famous line of Ruth as a pledge to Naomi, *"Your people will be my people, your God will be my God,"(1:16).* The book of Ruth is a story of friendship between two women and how they overcame the odds of life and survived.

The Book of Daniel

The first six chapters of this book are a collection of stories of Daniel's life and his friends who were taken into exile in Babylon. They became important government officials and at the same time, their faith in God were greatly tested. If you are going to read Daniel's story in the Bible, here is a rundown of what you will find and learn from Daniel's prayerful nature.

- Daniel's training in Babylon. He and his friends refused the food offered by the King as a sign of loyalty to Jewish's food.

- Daniel and friends were thrown in the burning furnace but they remained unhurt.

- Daniel was thrown into the lion's den after he was caught praying to God and remained unhurt.

The Revelation

This comes from the Greek word apokalypsis, meaning the unveiling or revealing. War, famine, disaster - the final book of the Bible shows how God brings about an end to evil and prepares a new city of love and peace for His chosen people. This is the only book in the Bible that is made up of apocalyptic writing. The visions are expressed in many symbols, shapes of animals, beasts, colors, and numbers among others with their corresponding secret meanings. Reading this book will leave you confused, but take comfort that these visions are intended to give hope and strengthen one's faith in God.

Chapter 10 – Step 10 – Know the Role of the Church in Your Walk with Jesus

The church is Jesus' bride. Marriage's symbolism is applied to Jesus and the body of believers. In the New Testament, Jesus, the Bridegroom, has chosen the church to become His bride. Similar today, the betrothal period during the biblical times was that the bride and groom were separated from each other until they walk down the aisle and wed, so is the bride of Christ, separated from His bridegroom. Now, the Church, as the bride, has the responsibility to be faithful to Him. When is the wedding? It will take place in the Second Coming of the Lord Jesus Christ. Such beautiful union of finally being one – Christ and His bride, the Church, an Eternal Union in Heaven.

All these, you will eventually know and understand if you read the Bible. And, what better way to fully understand the Word of God but to belong in a Church and be with other believers. The significance? You will get to have an in-depth understanding of the Scriptures you find confusing and be able to get the opinion of other believers and even the elders to shed light on some grey areas.

The following are some of the benefits of being a Church member as you continue to walk faithfully with Jesus and know His word:

1. Personal and spiritual development –

    Becoming a member of a church helps in your development as an individual. The church offers discipleship and spiritual development. You no longer be reading and reflecting on the Bible alone, you have the Church to guide you through every step of the way.

2. You get to join a small group – this is similar to having not just Bible buddies but also a spiritual family where you expect to grow more in the likeness of Jesus. The good thing about focused groups is that it is way easier to reach your goals of fully understanding the Bible and get to know God more because you are surrounded by people who have the same goals as yours.

3. A deep sense of belongingness – the church identifies you as a believer in Jesus Christ. As the Apostle Paul has written in his letter to the Ephesians, ""You are no longer strangers

and foreigners. You are citizens along with all of God's holy people. You are members of God's family." – Ephesians 2:19. With a deep sense of belongingness comes distinction. As a believer in Jesus Christ, you are different in the sense that you are committed to Christ's bride as evident to your being a member of the church. Along with becoming a member of the church is to personally confess your faith in the Lord Jesus, to be baptized in water and openly identify yourself as one with Christ. A church's membership is like saying, "I'm serious with my walk with the Lord and I'm not ashamed of claiming the one and only begotten son, Jesus Christ as my Lord and Savior."

4. You get to have encouragement like no other – Your walk with the Lord is not always a bed of roses, there will be times when you will falter. Even godly Christians and those who have been walking with the Lord for many years still experience spiritual dryness. It is but

normal, as we are only humans. But know that when you are a member of a church, its main role is to provide continuous encouragement to believers in living life on a daily basis. It is not just about getting by each day, but getting as much as you can out of the situation given you. If you have a spiritual family, you are assured that you will have a hand to pull you up when spiritual drought comes and arms to help keep you going. When you get tired pf reading the Bible, you have a church to provide encouragement and light to just keep reading and moving forward. As I Corinthians 12:4-7 would put it "A spiritual gift is given to each of us as a means of helping the entire church."

5. You are offered spiritual protection – Admit it, the world you live in is filled with evil ways. People now shifted their priorities to worldly matters and guarding their souls has not become a top priority. When you belong to a church and the Bible has become your basis to living, you are assured that there will be people who will watch over your soul and will keep you on the right track. One of the church's goals is to keep a close watch at your

soul. As the Apostle Paul said, "As each part does its own special work, it helps the other parts grow...."

6. A church helps you develop a Christ-like attitude – with the Bible as your guide and your Church as your spiritual support, developing a Christ-like attitude is achievable. A true follower of Jesus no longer lives for himself, but for the good of others. You become selfless and no longer concern yourself with personal issues. Instead, you become more aware of other's needs and welfare.

As true believers and followers of Jesus, it is not enough that we read the Bible, but it is also of prime importance that you read and understand His word together with your fellow believers.

As believers in Christ, we, the church, considered as the bride of Jesus, wait on great anticipation that soon we will be reunited with our Bridegroom, just as He promised. Until then, we remain faithful to Him, fulfill His purpose in our lives, and become like Him 'till we become one with the Lord for all eternity.

Chapter 11 – Step 11 - Some Additional Tips to Understand the Bible

This final chapter of the book provides you with some more tips to understand the Bible. So read wisely and learn from God's Word:

1. Fully surrender to God and make His Word rule over your life. This may not be easy but you must forsake your own ways, and be careful not to be misled by what the society dictates. Instead, do as God says, no matter how difficult it may seem to be, even without any assurance. Remember that God is in control. If you fully surrender to the Lord, He will surely direct your ways. If you surrender to Him, His Word will come alive and will become evident in your life.

2. Humble yourself before the Lord and ask Him for guidance – You'll know you are guided by the Spirit of God if you receive His Word and be able to interpret its true meaning. It is the Holy Spirit who makes the Word understandable for someone who earnestly studies and seeks His ways.

3. Be teachable - Remember the formula in approaching the Bible – right attitude, right spirit, and your willingness to be reproved. When you read the Bible, do so without prejudice. And be very cautious in proving all things.

4. Study the Bible on your knees – Not literally, but through prayer. Ask for wisdom, and you will be surprised how God gives it to people who earnestly and humbly seek Him. Remember, God is as close to you as you imagine Him to be. "If any of you lack wisdom, let him ask of God" (James 1:5).

5. Be sure to read the whole context – Avoid selective reading. Some Christians would read their Bible just so they could say that they have read it without really knowing what the verses truly mean. When you read, study the whole context and mull over the whole thought. You have to realize that divided verses are only for a reader's convenience. So make sure you read the whole chapter or the book.

6. Study the books written one at a time – do not be in a rush to read and finish the Bible because it will never be good for your soul. You will only end up confused and consumed. Study one passage or chapter at a time. And, make it a habit to find relative topics or passages from the Bible. You may use marginal references. Remember that everything written in the Bible has a connection, so make sure you find them in the different parts of the Bible.

7. Read the Bible as a two-way conversation – Just as a good communication is all about, reading the Bible is likewise a two-way street. You read and you also get to listen to Him. Imagine having a daily meeting with God. Imagine Him teaching you His Word. Doing so gives you the feeling of just having daily conversations with the Lord. This is much easier than stressing yourself out in trying to understand the Bible.

8. Read it because you wanted to learn more about Jesus – You have to realize your purpose for reading the Bible. Why do you

want to read from cover to cover? Set your purpose for doing so. Read because you wanted to know more about the One Messiah that God has sent to this world. You wanted to know his teachings and be able to apply them in your daily lives. If your purpose is Jesus, you are on the right track.

9. If you fully understand the Bible, you will be able to share the Good News to others by conducting a Bible study– the benefit of reading and fully understanding the Bible is that you will get the chance to share what you have read to others and be able to share to others through constant meeting to have a bible study. As you grow maturely in spirit through the help of your group, notice how you change perspective in the process – positive, more mature, and understanding.

10. The Bible is God's instructional manual to humans – Reading and understanding the Bible will allow people to know what God would really want His people to do. Everything you need to know is written in the

Bible, every question is answered by the Bible. What more can you ask for?

As you follow the steps provided here, you must realize that you should live what the Bible says and what the Lord tells you to do. Remember, God rewards obedience. He is always in control and is always on time. He created you for a purpose and He has good plans for you.

CONCLUSION

I hope this book was able to help you uncover the ways to read and understand the Bible and get to know the living God. The Lord has waited for you to come to this point of seeking Him. He has waited so long that He designed the day you opened your Bible as a turning point of your life. And so, it is comforting to know that we are loved by an infinite God, the most powerful, ever gracious Almighty we sometimes forget and take for granted.

The next step is to show your love to Him by reading His Word, which He made available to us. The Lord is worthy of your praise. He deserves your very best, your utmost reverence, and your all. Do not disappoint Him. Instead, share this book to others and transform into becoming more like Jesus. As you do so, remember that you are giving your one true God all the glory that He deserves.

Thank you and good luck!

Julia

More Best Selling Christian Titles:

Get All 3 Bible Study for Beginner Series Books in 1 spot:

1. The Bible for Beginners - 11 Easy Steps to Understanding the Bible & Becoming Closer to Christ in the Process...

2. How to Memorize The 25 Bible PRAYERS That EVERY Christian NEEDS to Know...

3. How to Memorize the 25 VERSES That EVERY Christian NEEDS to Know...

If you've always wanted to develop your prayer life, this book will teach you everything you need to know about prayer. From what prayer can teach us about God, to effective memorization techniques.

Now you have a chance to understand how to memorize the most important prayers that will have the most profound effect on your life...

Reading the Bible is the key to having a deeper understanding of our Christian faith. Because of the vastness of the book, it can be difficult to know exactly where to focus the bulk of your time. Some may argue that you need to understand the entire scripture, which in a normal day to day life, is nearly impossible.

Now you have a chance to understand how to memorize the most important verses that will have the most profound effect on your life...

13876607R00047

Printed in Great Britain
by Amazon.co.uk, Ltd.,
Marston Gate.